Here and Now

Also by Cynthia Hallam and published by Ginninderra Press

Bread and Butter People
Rising to the Occasion
Town Life
Living in the Moment
Moving with the Times
New Horizons

Cynthia Hallam

Here and Now

Acknowledgements

As always, my heartfelt thanks to my daughter Trish Farmer for her editing and unfailing support, Warren Nicholls, Roz Vrielink and Peter Miller for having kept the wheels of our writing group turning, Stephen Matthews for his continued belief in what I do, and remembering Deb Westbury, brilliant poet, mentor and friend, who always encouraged me to keep on writing.

To Trish, Michael and Ben

with love

Here and Now
ISBN 978 1 76041 624 9
Copyright © text Cynthis Hallam 2018
Copyright © cover photo Ginninderra Press

First published 2018 by
GINNINDERRA PRESS
PO Box 3461 Port Adelaide 5015 Australia
www.ginninderrapress.com.au

Contents

On the Coast	7
Windfall	8
Superiority	9
Flawless	10
Browsing	11
Light Entertainment	12
Here and Now	13
Clouds	14
Resurrection	15
Thankless	16
Indignation	17
Comeuppance	18
Horoscopes	20
Haven	21
Go Oscar!	23
Ordinary Days	24
Brushtails	25
Mangoes	26
Illusion	27
Befuddled	28
Caution	29
Attitudes	30
Numbers	31
Grieving	32
Heat	33
A Motorway Mystery	34
The Cure	35
Prima Donna	36
Pre-packaging	37
A Near Miss	38

A Change of Tenancy	39
Travelling	40
Anguish	41
Perception	42
A Haiku Sextet	43
The Entertainers	44
A Surprising Excursion	45
Suspicion	46
Tempest	47
Innovations	48
Perseverance	49
A January Reflection	50
Seasons	51
Unity	52
Community	53
Pleasures	54
Old Faithful	55
A Sonnet to Winter	56
The Holiday From Hell	57
Anticipation	58
Flowering	59
A Fairy Tale Ending	60

On the Coast

Today, the sea and sky are sapphire blue,
a hint of approaching spring and benign surf
luring intrepid swimmers
to join the usual joggers on the beach
much earlier than might have been expected.

While last week, the death throes of winter
brought only leaden skies, an uninviting chop
and deceptive rips,
somehow, this morning's unexpected promise
is already diffusing past disappointments
as we experience once again
the tingling delight of an incoming tide
eddying around the sand between our toes
and anticipate the warmer pleasures coming.

Windfall

It is weightless,
so small, it fits snugly in my palm,
the delicate, intricate work of art
a testimony to skill and perseverance.

The nest, blown from its moorings
onto the lawn by an angry wind
has my awed admiration
that such a complex, king-size project
for a miniature builder
is constructed with such expertise.

Perhaps, somewhere in the foliage,
a tiny bird is mourning its loss
but, unable to effect any restitution
I can only hold it up
to facilitate a final viewing
and reassure a bereft little architect
that its inspirational masterpiece
will still be valued.

Nest identified as probably a striated thornbill's

Superiority

Everyone knows that I am highly intelligent,
that we felines are the sharpest species on the planet
(will any ignorant homo sapiens please take note)
but if you still want proof, it is obvious on a daily basis.

The members of my household have the mistaken belief
that they are calling the shots
yet who opens doors on demand to usher me in or out?
Who cleans out my litter box? (Mieeuw!)
Whose bed has pride of place in front of the fire
when the weather turns chilly?
Who rolls the ping-pong ball when I feel like a game
and gives me regular manicures and full-body brushes?
(Really, all that fuss about a few hairs and tears
is just a power trip for those who are less blessed!)

So, while they are out on some puerile, human errand,
I might treat my bored palate to a quality snack
and if I can claw the stupid lid off this can of salmon
my day, like me, will be absolutely purrfect.

Flawless

He's a master of perfection.
Everything by the book,
exact in every detail.
His physique
is remarkable for his age,
clothes immaculate,
impeccably tailored,
his car
in pristine condition
with never a speck of dust
to defile its shine.

He is always on time,
business affairs
infallibly in faultless order,
all in the firm belief
that perfection
is the secret of success.
In fact,
he's so busy being perfect
there is no time left
for anything else
which appears to be
perfectly fine by him!

Browsing

The mountain villages are much the same
with their sprinkling of retailers
catering to the daily needs of the locals
and an eclectic array of coffee shops, cafes,
antique and 'pre-loved' establishments
to lure the lifeblood of the area. Tourists!

Trading times are conventionally set
by the daylight hours of the current season
except a shop open 'when we feel like it'
(according to the notice on the door)
which never seems to coincide
with whenever I find myself in the vicinity.

So being frustratingly thwarted again
I peer through the window's congestion
at the huge collection of who knows what,
hoping that when I am next passing by
I can go inside to satisfy my curiosity,
even find something I never knew I wanted.

Light Entertainment

Why is it
that whenever I am driving
and time is of the essence
the lights
conspire against me?
When I have wisely allowed
for any traffic delays
I am ushered along my way
so smoothly
I arrive at a destination
embarrassingly, too early.

When rarely
I turn up at the proper time
my euphoria lasts
until I journey home
and join the queue at a red,
proceed on the green,
then thwarted by
amber's too brief invitation
come to a jarring halt,
confirming
what I have long suspected.

Those lights
remember my number plate
and fiddle the cycle,
for my frustration
is the highlight of their day!

Here and Now

At this precise moment in time
we are a sum of the choices we have made,
decisions put into action by circumstance,
our physiological inheritance,
but our lives are still constantly changing.

Second chances can be better than the first,
new possibilities may fulfil our dreams,
unexpected challenges will test our mettle,
and things happen beyond our control,
so we need to make the most of it,
this here and now marking time at our feet,
and be thankful, that shaped by our past,
we are better prepared to tackle the future.

Clouds

They have blown across
from a rapidly darkening western horizon
on a fitful wind
eddying haphazardly through the garden eucalypts
as if searching for a direction in which to go.
The clear, azure backdrop of the sky
that held such promise for a perfect spring day
has been hijacked by an unexpected weather event
not forecast by any gurus in the media
who are relied on for their climate expertise.

I await the arrival of the burgeoning storm
after a hasty retrieval of garden chairs
and a line of washing not yet dry,
but instead, the sun is reappearing,
and the wind, gusting now with renewed purpose
is herding the clouds away,
apparently, just pausing in my neighbourhood
for its bearings,
and having sorted out where it should be heading
has resumed the journey to the coast.

Resurrection

Abandoned for as long as I can remember,
the old place down the street has come to life.
A bike with training wheels, a scooter, skipping rope
lie strewn over the front lawn
and a freshly washed car is dripping in the drive.

Windows have been thrown open to the breeze
and down the side passage
there's a glimpse of sheets flapping on the line.
A dozing cat, already settled in,
shares the doormat with a pair of shoes.

A faint clatter of crockery and family conversation
wafts towards me from inside
and I can't help smiling as I continue my walk,
a hint of new growth in the hedge
echoing my relief and delight in the revival

Thankless

From the verge where boys are playing
on their way home from school,
a ball heads towards my car
and the catcher
backs onto the road to receive it.
My seat belt crushes me
in a swift, bruising embrace
as I floor the brakes
and the car behind nudges my bumper.

The boy regains his feet
and, his credibility before his peers
apparently the only casualty,
glares accusingly through my windscreen
and pokes out his tongue.
Retrieves the ball from under the car
to resume their game
but his mates have already disappeared
so he takes off,
a single finger raised in my direction.

Behind me,
a string of after-school traffic banks up,
horns bleating
as gingerly, I step outside
to deal with my own situation.
Pay the price for unappreciated diligence.

Indignation

This year, her club's charity auction
has attracted the usual array of bric-a-brac
and she is enjoying inspecting the collection,
wondering why anyone in their right mind
had acquired some of it in the first place!

But she stops in her tracks when she finds
the lava lamp she donated last year
tucked behind a hideous set of canisters.
Honestly, she fumes inside, these days
people just can't seem to appreciate class
and when it is auctioned again later on
she would vastly outbid all the other offers
so that whoever had foolishly returned it
will be absolutely mortified
that they'd had no concept of its value!

Comeuppance

In the crowded car park,
an upmarket limousine
is centred over two spaces
and I crawl past,
parkless and frustrated,
seething with indignation.

I cruise the circuit again
but approaching
the altar of selfishness
my righteous wrath
morphs into amusement
as I observe the driver,
(wearing sunglasses
on a dull, cloudy day,)
hastily loading
a mega pack of toilet rolls
into the open boot.

I cannot help myself,
brazenly blasting my horn
and he turns, startled,
but relieved, no doubt,
that no one he knows
has witnessed the need
to accommodate
his use of a bathroom.

Pleased by his discomfort,
I smile as I am circling
to claim one of his spots
but two usurpers
are already pulling in
and with some contrition
try to convince myself
that I didn't want
to go shopping anyway.

Horoscopes

The first thing I look at
in a paper or magazine
is my stars,
believing in the good,
rereading them
to reinforce my smile,
and ignoring the bad
as being of no account.

Yet, I must confess,
when astrologers
from other sources
have a different view
of my future
I take a sensible option
and dismiss it all
as a load of rubbish.

But the following week,
the first thing I look at
in a paper or magazine
is my stars.

Haven

Nestled in the shadow of the mountains,
our town is quite lively for a midweek morning.
Coffee shops are doing steady business,
the supermarket car park is more than half full.
Even the pub veranda is hosting customers,
a trio of motorbikes
lined up like alien soldiers at the kerb.

As usual, the man and his singing dog
are sharing a rug outside the pharmacy,
the dog's paw resting on a cap
with a few coins and today, a five-dollar note!
A small child, holding her mother's hand
is having a one-sided conversation with the dog
who is listening with a soppy grin.

Some of the hairdresser's chairs are occupied,
and next door among the posters,
the travel agent is mesmerising an elderly couple
with the delights of Bali on her screen.
The bank's tellers are dealing with a queue.

Knowing that the young Buddhist monk
who appears at the bus stop from time to time
will politely decline any offers of money,
I buy a sultana bun for his breakfast
and I am rewarded
with a warm smile and blessing for my trouble.

On a high, I pass the newsagent's magazine display,
reminded that life in our township
is small potatoes in the wider scheme of things
but as far as I'm concerned,
its living, breathing tapestry is a banquet
with a generous serve of contentment on the side.

Go Oscar!

Resisting enticement
can be quite challenging,
testing our self-control
(or not)
when at times we are feeling
that plenty is not enough
and become a glutton
over the self-serve pavlova,
for as Mae West
once famously proclaimed,
'too much of anything
can be wonderful!'

Caving in can provide
a much more satisfying high
than a sense of
righteous superiority
after forgoing
a desirable opportunity,
and is a great way to revive
an otherwise dull day,
emulating Oscar Wilde
who happily boasted that
he could resist anything
but temptation.

Ordinary Days

Outside, the weather is bleak and uncertain.
The sky is leaden, cloudy, but there's no sign of rain
yet somehow, a gloomy, creeping damp
already mists the windows
forestalling any desire to encounter the breeze
fondling the stillness with icy fingers.

Hour by hour, our usual routine progresses,
the atmosphere idling in neutral.
A day when nothing outstanding commends it
or marks its passing
when more exciting times are being remembered.

Nothing of importance has called for our attention
beyond the boundaries of our regular agenda.
Anything of unusual interest
has eluded any conscious recognition.
Just another unremarkable, nondescript day
that in time and unnoticed, will fade into oblivion.

Brushtails

The resident possum mafia
has been at it again,
my crop of sweet Meyer lemons
ambushed and half eaten,
then scattered in careless abandon
all over the backyard.
And this time, some pot plants
have been bowled over!
Little vandals!

I'm a confirmed animal lover
but now at the end of my tether.
My fruit and blossom trees
and whatever I plant
have been fair game for too long,
and I may have to abort my defence
if I can't come up
with a more effective strategy.
But what?

Hang on, I've just remembered
that a while ago
I was sent from New Zealand
some lovely fluffy, warm socks.
'Made from genuine possum fur'
the Kiwi label boasted,
and THAT'S a win-win solution
well worth thinking about.
Isn't it?

Mangoes

Those harbingers of summer expectations
are now arriving in the shops
to join the other so-called tropical fruits
that never seem to be out of season.

That sticky juice trickling down your arm
no matter how carefully you bite
and sliver of fibre stuck between your teeth
are no barrier to arousing dreams
of waving palms, an inviting surf rolling in.
A celebration for your taste buds
that lingers long after you've cleaned up.

Eating a mango is a special experience
that absorbs your whole attention,
a delightful feast that sometimes, has you
slowing down to prolong the pleasure,
for no other fruit can ever aspire
to being quite as seductively delicious.

Illusion

Viewed from the mountain escarpment,
a carpet of city lights stretches to the far horizon,
the radiant full moon and tapestry of stars
painting everything with a benign ambience,
camouflaging the reality of modern living.

A police siren is wailing somewhere on the plains.
A blaring ambulance copes with another crisis,
one of their never ending nightly dramas.
Flashing lights are converging on a nearby street
and in the distance, something is on fire.

The visual magic of the panorama begins to fade
as I realise that under the glittering façade,
elements of the human condition are changing.
Lives are coming to an end, others just beginning.
Relationships are irrevocably breaking down,
others celebrating new commitments.

Ordinary lives are being carelessly overtaken
by circumstances that are beyond their control.
Other futures turned upside down
by someone else's late-night misjudgement
and sadly, no stars or moonlight in the morning
to smooth away all the frayed edges.

Befuddled

'Easy. You can't miss it,'
the man on the footpath said.
'Turn left at the lights,
right at Maccas
then left at the nursery.
Turn right at the garage,
left past the timber yard
until the roundabout,
right until the next lights
then right again
and it's opposite the pub.'

Pleased that he has helped
he gives a cheerful wave
as I smile my thanks
and head into the traffic.
Now, what was that again?
Right at the lights…

Caution

Like many others, my life is littered with
would'ves, could'ves and should'ves
but second thoughts won't change a thing
to improve my current situation
or line up with my new positive thinking
about no regrets.

I will start having a go at some 'why nots',
pluck up the courage
to jump in without too much thought.
Spontaneously take a leap of confidence,
relying at last, on my so called
'natural instincts.'

I will try sticking my neck out for once,
sign up for that mystery tour
and let the adrenalin blow me away.
But perhaps that's a bit TOO impetuous
so I should probably give it a miss.
Maybe next time.

Attitudes

I draw to a halt at the pedestrian crossing
while two of the current, entitled generation
stroll across absorbed in their phones,
in the firm belief that as a protected species,
painted lines
will cocoon them from any harm.

Just behind, an elderly couple smile and wave
and with enormous pleasure I respond,
glad that we of the older generation
who grew up learning basic good manners,
can still enjoy
human to human communication.

Later, I step onto the crossing at the shops,
waving to the waiting, grey-haired driver,
smugly expecting the usual reply
but like a thunderbolt out of a clear blue sky
he glares at me and then turns away,
my rusted on theory rocking to the core
as I hurry on,
realigning my former perspective.

Numbers

Age or value do not come into the equation
in her growing obsession with 'Street Appeal',
habitually assessing the real estate
on her frequent, increasingly far-ranging walks.

Charmed by the 9 out of 10 decades-old originals
with well-kept, mature gardens
and the classic, California Bungalows.
The delightfully quirky 8 with a flock of galahs
painted on one of the windows
and a pair of magpies on the letter box.
The sweet 7.5 being restored with sensitivity,
an appealing, rebuild 8.5 that surprisingly, fits in.

Disappointed by a possible 7, downgraded
for its permanently visible rubbish bins,
the 6s with garage doors dominating the façade
and clusters of newly built, impersonal clones.
Some 4.5s with badly-matched extensions
or overwhelmed by tangled greenery.
The zero out of 10 duplex on a narrow block
presenting a graceless, windowless, garage wall.

But although she is enjoying each new challenge,
the greatest pleasure is to arrive back
at her own front gate to view, in her firm opinion,
the only 10 out of 10 in the neighbourhood.

Grieving

It is clear that she is still missing the sister
who for years had been her companion
but succumbed to illness a few months ago.
Again, she is demanding I open
the bedroom cupboard where near the end
her sibling hid her indisposition,
to sniff any lingering bond
that only littermates can recognise.

In sympathy, I gather her in my arms,
wishing I was fluent in feline conversation,
gratified that at least,
a faint purr is acknowledging my intent
but the chubby old mourner wriggles free
and heads for the kitchen door,
comfort from her bowl of nibbles
the preferred consolation for her loss.

Heat

Today, is what in technical circles
they call a stinker.
The overhead fans have been on all night
and continue churning warm, humid air
in futile eddies through the house.

Earlier, I ventured outside
to give drooping plants the will to live,
top up the bird bath and the saucer
for our resident family of lizards
but didn't encounter the usual birds
who, wise to Mother Nature's intention
have already retired
to the shelter of the eerily still trees.

So, with outdoor activities now on hold
and not requiring to adhere
to any necessary, regular routine,
I can indulge in the day of guiltless sloth
that a heatwave can always justify.

A Motorway Mystery

With an anxious concentration,
the grey haired man clutches the wheel
and with an element of surprise
I observe the P plates as he is passing
and cannot help wondering why.

Did he previously lose his licence
because of a drunken misdemeanour?
Never learned to drive before
and his bucket list is now shorter?
Has he been away, spent time in gaol
or simply going for a bit of a run
in a grandson's latest pride and joy?
Then again, he may have stolen it!

I hear an insistent, tooting horn
and in my rear vision mirror see a ute
is tailgating the very nervous driver
and with some concern for his welfare
hope that, whatever his situation,
the mature novice isn't unduly rattled
and safely reaches his destination.

The Cure

Suffering from rainy day blues,
the woman halts her car at the crossing
where a small girl
protected by galoshes and umbrella
splashes in the gutter's flow,
totally absorbed in her delight,
oblivious of her precarious location.

The mother reaches the opposite kerb
with a younger child
and aware the other isn't by her side
hastens back and takes her hand.
Shepherds her across,
apologising to the waiting driver
who is still smiling as she moves on,
the magic of such innocent joy
stoking the embers of her fading spirits,
defusing her indisposition.

Prima Donna

In the supermarket,
the burly, tattooed man and I
stand side by side in the pet food aisle,
surveying the array of food for cats.
With concentration, he searches
the most expensive brand
while my purchases are more modest.

I remark with a smile 'Fussy cat, eh?'
and he holds up his selections.
'Fussy!' he grins, with obvious affection.
'She's made it very clear
what she WILL eat and what she won't,
the little madam,'
and the vision of a small, bossy feline
cuddling up to those incredible tattoos
just makes my day
and has me smiling, all the way home.

Pre-packaging

It is getting so much harder
to access some of our day-to-day purchases.
The machines that encase merchandise
for the retailers' shelves
are rendering it impossible for human hands
to negotiate without a jackhammer,
a Stanley knife, razor blade or spanner.

The way things seem to be going,
new work opportunities may well arise,
people we can hire to open up the shopping
when we get back home,
experts with all the necessary equipment
for putting on the pressure required
to alleviate the nation's packaging crisis.

Unemployment levels would come down.
The need to call in paramedics
after a grim attempt to get at the batteries
could be eliminated
and scarce medical resources freed up.
Recyclers will process more blood-free plastic
and consumers would be forever grateful.

A Near Miss

Everyone stops whatever they are doing
when they hear the fire station's warning siren
for as feared, the unpredictable wind has changed course
and the bushfire is now headed in their direction.

Experienced in the reality of country town summers,
plans of action are already being put into place
as shops and businesses are secured,
children picked up from school and homes prepared.
Guttering is filled with water against flying embers,
outdoor furniture stored inside, the washing brought in.
Vehicles are being packed with irreplaceables,
changes of clothes, carriers ready for pets
in case a last minute retreat becomes necessary.

Then against all odds, the wind loses its momentum,
until finally reversing over the charred bush
taking its cargo of smoke and uncertainty along for the ride
and the siren confirms that the danger has passed.

With collective relief, lives ease back to normal
and later, there'll be a beer at the club with the volunteers,
still on call in case they are needed somewhere else,
thankful that today, mother nature was in their corner.

A Change of Tenancy

The bush block over the road
has just been cleared
to build a new dwelling,
the only vacant lot
in our neighbourhood
taking a deafening five days
to be reduced to
almost tennis court status.

In the temporary calm,
two kookaburras are sitting
hunched and silent
on the dividing fence,
no doubt contemplating
the human logic
of demolishing their home
to erect another,
and obviously concluding
that it is no laughing matter.

Travelling

Circle the Australian coastline in a mobile home.
Go on a photo safari in a game park in Africa.
Dine and see a show at the Moulin Rouge in Paris
and the Guard changing at Buckingham Palace.
Done that.

Sip hot toddies by a chalet fire in the Swiss Alps.
Explore inside a pyramid and the sphinx.
Journey by train through the Canadian Rockies
and cruise some of the European rivers.
Done that.

Go sailing on a yacht around the Pacific islands.
Be at Anzac Cove in Turkey on Anzac Day.
Check all my aspirations are on the bucket list
and nothing significant has been left off.
Just done that.

Anguish

She is walking along the footpath at the shops,
tears in her eyes as frantically,
she keys the device in her palm
oblivious to the pedestrians stepping aside
as she blunders on.
What has caused the teenager's desperation?
Being bullied? Failed a vital exam?
Or maybe a boyfriend is wanting to break up.

Concerned and before I lose her in the crowd,
I consider following to see if I can help
but realise, that in these days
of changing times and generations
such an intimate intervention by a stranger
might not be welcomed
and can only hope that somewhere,
familiar arms are waiting to give her comfort.

Perception

Everyone says that old Maggie is eccentric
but I'm not altogether sure about that.
She colour matches pegs to the washing,
uses an umbrella heedless of the weather
and five cats might be a bit over the top.

Winter or summer,
she always wears a woolly cap and boots,
keeps her windows permanently open,
and often plays the piano and sings
at full throttle from the old-time musicals.

I suppose that everything might be true
but she has such a spring in her step
and always seems so happy with her lot
that sometimes, if the truth be known,
while we laugh about her on the outside,
we are feeling a secret twinge of envy.

A Haiku Sextet

Moonlight bathes a spire,
sunset's hint of warmth now spent.
Owls are out hunting.

A love song wafts through
the balmy, autumn evening.
A heartbeat quickens.

Joyful dolphins ride
a surging, storm-driven swell.
Grounded gulls bicker.

Winter sunshine glows,
warming sad and chilly thoughts.
Birds ascend singing.

A freesia blossom
nods in the late winter breeze.
Out too soon, but proud.

Spring is nearly here.
Its promise hangs temptingly.
Morning frosts linger.

The Entertainers

Like clowns under a big top,
the kittens hold our amused attention
as they trip over ping pong balls,
pounce on invisible mice
then collapse in a tangle of legs
not yet fully accustomed to
the rigours of rough and tumble play.

They are not seasoned performers
yet the pratfalls and double takes
in their encounter with a feather,
bungled ambush on a ball of wool
and skittering, skidding chase
are equally as entertaining for
their innocent, spontaneous charm.

But, barely more than infants,
their reserve of energy is limited
so instead of a drink in the caravan
to wind down after a show,
they will sleep it off in their basket
and emerge, batteries charged, for
their next appearance in the limelight.

A Surprising Excursion

Her first inter-urban train trip for a while
is certainly becoming a revelation
for the expected relaxing hour into the city
has been getting a bit unnerving
because of all those confronting signs!

'Move to next carriage if danger is present.'
'Use alarm button to alert crew.'
'Security cameras may be in use'
and 'Police regularly patrol the train.'
The 'Cover your cough or sneeze please',
'Keep it clean', 'Don't leave litter',
and warning to 'Keep your feet off the seat'
have been reduced to insignificance.

At passing stations, she looks for reassurance
to allay her growing disquiet
but the 'Emergency Help Point' signs
advising that 'In most emergency situations
it is safer to remain on the train'
are doing nothing to soothe her anxiety.

Across the aisle, a youth in a black hoody
keeps a hand suspiciously in his pocket
so just in case, she hides her wallet
under the umbrella in the bottom of her bag
and remains vigilant
until she steps onto the platform at Central,
composure restored by her survival.

Suspicion

For quite some time now, a For Sale sign
has remained on the house around the corner,
unusual in this age of real estate mania.
Is the purchase price overambitious?
Are termites undermining the foundations?
Galloping mould invading the ceilings?
Is a sink hole developing in the backyard
or some bullet holes in the front door
courtesy of a previous owner's connections?

Yet the location is very family friendly,
schools and transport conveniently nearby,
the shops just a comfortable walk away,
an inviting park and playground close by.
In fact, the advertised 'desirable property'
that I'd be tempted to buy myself.
Then again, on second thoughts, maybe not.

Tempest

Ominous clouds have kidnapped a sunny afternoon
and I am listening to the storm,
waves of rain surfing across the corrugated roof,
primeval thunder as nature's aggravation
grumbles overhead
after the power-filled flashes of targeted electricity.

I remain suspended, aware of my insignificance
while it vents its fury
then as swiftly as it has taken charge, it moves on,
leaving overflowing gutters in the street,
gurgling downpipes, dripping trees
and benign, emerging sunshine to mark its passing.

Innovations

The new coffee shop in town is offering
peanut butter and banana smoothies
and inviting us to warm up
with a turmeric and beetroot latte.
They are kidding right?
Apparently not, for there are people inside
and none of them are looking unhappy.

But wimp that I am, I pass on by
for my usual cappuccino and raisin toast
which somehow today,
seem to have lost their flavour,
are not as appealing,
and find myself wishing that my taste buds
were not so stubbornly conservative.

Perseverance

Living in a gap between aspiration and achievement,
she leads an 'I'll be happy when' existence,
all that happens now, never quite measuring up
to the standard of her imagined nirvana.
Possibilities come and go but to her,
never feeling 'right' enough to explore any potential.

She can still attract her share of romance
but won't commit in case another is more suitable,
a knight in shining armour
who will fit more perfectly into her fantasies.
Her job is as banal as a skinny, decaf latte
but rejects any exciting new positions
for there may be a better one just around the corner.

So as usual, the days in her life keep on drifting along,
ignoring the golden opportunities,
skimming through an irrelevant here and now.
Rationalising all her decisions
before retreating into dreams of what is to come
when her 'happy ever after' finally becomes a reality.

A January Reflection

Finally,
after too many weeks of fevered anticipation,
Christmas is as far away as ever.
Along the main street,
the strings of bunting have been taken down,
shop windows divested of their tinsel.

At home,
twinkling extravaganzas are being dismantled,
wilting trees bundled outside
or returned, shedding plastic, to the garage.
Decorations packed away
until their next, sentimental appearance.

Again,
family dynamics were brought into focus.
The awkward, changed relationships,
joyful reunions, embarrassing overindulgences,
delightful or disastrous holidays.
The lonely, just wanting the season over.

But now,
in the relative peace of these late January days
our interest can turn to other things
until those cunning shops surprise us all
with October displays of mince pies,
jolting our festive spirit back into momentum.

Seasons

Today, we have had four seasons in one.
At the conjunction of summer and autumn
some inconsistency is expected
but this has been absolutely ridiculous.
Waking up to a chill
requiring the digging out of warm jackets,
then clouds roll in from nowhere
and a shower drenches the washing.

A blanket of humidity engulfs us
and starting to sweat, we resort to the fans
but then it disappears
as the clearest blue sky and gentle breeze
take the sting out of our impatience.

And now, enjoying a pleasant, balmy dusk
with our day of upheaval settling down,
it is a relief to know
that despite all the conflicting indications,
autumn has not really abandoned us.

Unity

Like a guard of honour against the country roadside fence,
ramshackle utes, family sedans and upmarket four-wheel drives
are baking in the summer sun.
On the far side of the field, time-worn headstones of pioneers
frame mourners, heads protected by Akubras bent
as a eulogy or prayer focuses their attention,
and I wonder who, in the sparseness of this rural domain,
has attracted such a remarkably diverse congregation.

Was it a well-known mayor, postmistress or district nurse
drawing such allegiance from the rich, poor and in-between
or someone, just rich in love for their fellow man,
poor in dispensing blame,
an impartial mentor who in wisdom had taken the middle road
when supporting all comers through conflict or travail
and has left a community in sorrow by their passing.

Community

As usual, Sunday in the car park at the shops is peaceful,
but yesterday, was bustling with carnival rides and shrieking kids,
the town alive with strolling families and their dogs,
couples holding hands and groups in animated conversation
enjoying the annual Foundation Day celebration
in perfect autumn weather.

Stalls lining the main street cooked aromatic, exotic food
beside the comfortably familiar,
others promoted local businesses, services and associations
while the district's artisans showed off their wares.
Entertainment from the stages competed for attention
with school choirs, jazz bands and an enthusiastic dancing group
encouraging a willing crowd to participate.
Even the dogs seemed to sense the party mood,
greeting each other with bottom sniffs and wagging tails
matching the universal, human smiles,
the pleasure of meeting old friends and encountering the new.

Like always, everything has been restored to normality overnight,
leaving a row of portaloos awaiting collection
and memories of a day of relaxation and communal goodwill
to warm us through the coming winter.

Pleasures

Softly as an angel's wing,
the winter evening
is closing in,
a fresh but gentle breeze
caressing my cheek
as contentedly,
I rake around the shrubs,
but much too soon,
the gathering shadows
overtake the yard
and the sudden chill
sends me scuttling inside,
to sit back and relax
with my favourite drink
by a cosy fire,
leaving the world outside
to sort its own version
of creature comfort.

Old Faithful

It is so ancient I have forgotten where I bought it
yet somehow, I can't seem to let it go.
Every winter for too many years
it has been thrown out in favour of several others
languishing in the wardrobe's depths
but is rescued, again and again, just in time.

The dressing gown has seen much better days,
seams constantly being restitched,
hem repaired with frustrating regularity.
Generations of cat hairs have been brushed off,
spillage and accidents washed out
during the usual, indispositions of winter.

Its bindings are fraying to the point of no return
yet here I am, still enjoying its cosy warmth,
the comfort of its history
as again, I have shrunk from its ultimate demise
and probably, when I meet my own,
I will be shrouded in its folds of green velour
so that together, we can journey into eternity.

A Sonnet to Winter

The winter chill refrigerates my bones,
a breeze right off the ice its constant mate,
there's not a single leaf on the maples
and shrubs are in a catatonic state.
The grass just looks like stubble not a lawn,
the bird bath's frozen over once again,
the washing won't dry without the dryer,
transporting bills to stratosphere's domain.
But the grass does not need any mowing
and all the weeds have given up the ghost,
hot beverages around a cosy fire
can substitute for ice cream on the coast.
And even if the ski slopes aren't our thing,
know each day is one day closer to spring.

The Holiday From Hell

The view from the room is a car park,
Hardly the advertised sea,
Even the pool's a disappointment,

Half what they reckoned it would be.
On the 'comfortable private balcony',
Lacking a single chair,
I've discovered this decomposed seagull
Defiling the surrounding air.
And the bed has got all these wrinkles,
You'd swear it's been slept in before,

For you'd never guess what's left behind
Right here on the floor.
Outside the rain is setting in,
Moaning wind chills from the shore and

Heaven forbid! The power's gone out,
Ending my desire to stay, for
Lord help me only a masochist, could
Live in this place any more!

Anticipation

Framed
in the pink lace
of early spring buds
on a tree
still bare of leaves,
a pair of
newly arrived
crimson rosellas
preen their feathers

Add the scent
of newborn freesias,
a drone
of distant mowing,
a tepid breeze,
and the promise
of warmer weather
just ahead
is very encouraging.

Flowering

As usual during the last week of August,
the only orchid in the garden
has produced a single spike of blooms,
delicate, golden petals unfolding
to reveal their russet-freckled tongues,
a pleasing surprise that
despite being pot-bound and neglected,
the Cymbidium has managed it again.

So as always on the first day of spring,
the stem has been displayed
on the windowsill in its special vase,
delighting us to the end of September,
when in slow progression,
the eight charmers will give their all
until next year, when with hope
and another promise of more attention
it will amaze us again,
encouraged by the last gasp of winter.

A Fairy Tale Ending

Now honestly, who on earth is this Cinderella
and what's all the fuss about that Jack fella,
just a silly kid with a fetish for beans
who grew one taller than your average greens.
Goldilocks sounds like a real hot doll
but is Red Riding Hood some bikie's moll?

Is Rapunzel an Ugly Duckling or Sleeping Beauty?
The Little Mermaid another Olympic cutie?
Are the Three Bears just boy-band jokes
and Snow White mates with seven small blokes?
Would a Princess really go to bed with a pea?
Well, it all seems pretty unlikely to me!

Rumpelstiltskin, Tom Thumb and a Frog Prince
would surely make any reader wince
and for heaven's sake, Three Billygoats Gruff?
I tell you, forget about all that stuff
for it's clear that these fables are all about
gross mega fantasies and too far out,
so take the advice that I have heard said.
and stick with reality on video games instead!

www.ingramcontent.com/pod-product-compliance
Lightning Source LLC
Chambersburg PA
CBHW070051120526
44589CB00034B/1911